Lydia, A Seller of Purple

TEACH Services, Inc.
P U B L I S H I N G
www.TEACHServices.com • (800) 367-1844

World rights reserved. This book or any portion thereof may not be copied or reproduced in any form or manner whatever, except as provided by law, without the written permission of the publisher, except by a reviewer who may quote brief passages in a review.

The author assumes full responsibility for the accuracy of all facts and quotations as cited in this book. The opinions expressed in this book are the author's personal views and interpretations, and do not necessarily reflect those of the publisher.

This book is provided with the understanding that the publisher is not engaged in giving spiritual, legal, medical, or other professional advice. If authoritative advice is needed, the reader should seek the counsel of a competent professional.

Copyright © 2005 TEACH Services, Inc.
ISBN-13: 978-1-57258-351-1 (Paperback)
Library of Congress Control Number: 20059318872005931887

Lydia,
A Seller Of Purple

By
Josephine Cunnington Edwards

REVIEW AND HERALD
PUBLISHING ASSOCIATION
WASHINGTON, D.C.

OFFSET IN U.S.A.

Lydia, A Seller of Purple

Lost Creek is such a merryhearted stream that it dimples and laughs aloud at the least little thing. Maybe it is because some blade of lush, long grass from the riverbank tickles its cheek; perhaps some dragonfly or insect skating across its clear surface makes it bubble in amusement. Or maybe it is jolly because it was such a blessing to the children in the tiny flag station of Mustardville in eastern Pennsylvania, for as it tumbled along behind the scattered houses the children waded and built dams in it from May till late September. Then, pretty soon Lost Creek's smile grew icy and rigid, and the children had to wait till spring came along to hear it laugh again.

Little Lydia Moore used to toddle down to the brook from the Moores' weatherbeaten house every day. There by the willows she would lay out tiny lanes and villages, and border them with pretty pebbles that she had washed clean in the brook. Then when Mother called her little brood to dinner she would gravely trot along with the rest, her tiny bare feet peeking out from under the long skirts that little girls wore in the 1880's.

Their house was tall, rawboned, and bare, and the strong winds had long ago whipped off the paint, leaving the timbers dry and warped.

In the long kitchen the great homemade table dominated the middle of the floor. Lydia still remembers the large loaves of bread, browned and odorous, that her mother served to them on the clean-scoured boards.

What if the dishes were but stained and checked old crockery, and the bone-handled steel knives were nicked and old? Never had anything tasted better to Lydia than the great bowls of mush eaten with rich milk, or the potatoes mashed or whipped till they were as white as the driven snow.

The years seemed to fly by; the events were like a vast, moving kaleidoscope to the girl. Days on end were spent in the stuffy, one-room brick schoolhouse, where Lydia caught not only her first taste and love of learning but the measles, mumps, and chickenpox as well.

And so the child had grown up—in simple, solid, plain surroundings, leaving behind her sweet memories of picnics down the branch, to which her mother would bring great baskets of food to please her little children.

Lydia could see her yet, puffing and panting, spreading the large white cloth on the ground under the tree that bends over the river. Then she would lift out great crocks of pickled beets and hard-boiled eggs; big light fluffy biscuits, and butter and jam; pans of baked beans and a crock of cottage cheese. She always baked a big buttermilk chocolate cake, rich with raisins.

Lydia could dimly remember the long, happy walk home, her tiny bare feet embedding themselves in the soft dust. Each child would carry something. Chester always carried the water bucket with the dipper clinking metallically against the side; Kathleen, the little milk bucket; and Lydia, the big shawl Mother always took to spread on the ground. Mother, big and plump, would follow the children.

Then one day Father was brought home, broken and bleeding from an accident on the section gang.

The long box, set for its brief stay in the front room, seemed oddly grand in the homely, plain old parlor. It had been covered with black felt, and the handles and hinges were silver.

Mother always kept the ingrain carpet spotless, and the old, mended Nottingham lace curtains were stiffly starched and snowy white. White tidies, crocheted from coarse thread, were pinned on the back of every rocker.

Then the room was full of awkward men clumping about in great greased boots, uncomfortable in good coats and neckties, and red-faced, tired women, looking only faintly feminine in misshapen rusty hats and neatly patched black dresses. Lydia could remember the parson from the old weatherbeaten church down the road preaching the funeral sermon. Then when they started to the cemetery, it began to rain—a cold, drenching, miserable rain. The pallbearers slipped and slid in the yellow clay as they bore their burden to the place prepared for it. There was little time for graveside rites. Finally, the little family was home again, and Mother, bereft as she was, began to scour the clumps of yellow clay out of her house. She could not bear dirt—any time, any place.

There was no use thinking about it, they could not stay in the big bleak house any longer. The only reason they had for being there was gone. It had been handy for Father's work, and now he would never again come home, grizzled and laughing, on the handcar. He had always run up the path with his old battered bucket, and scooping up the first child that came running to meet him, showered it with bristly, whiskery kisses.

But now he would come no more. Mother got great wooden boxes from the general store and began to pack. Sometimes Lydia heard her catch her breath on the crest of a sob. Then she would see her smoothing an old pair of woolen socks, folded into a neat ball, or a battered felt hat that she had taken down from a closet shelf.

They moved to the city of Philadelphia, into a big, square, many-windowed house set right on the edge of the sidewalk. Lydia's mother had chosen it with an eye to size and location, for she knew she must turn her hand to something to earn money for her growing family. Not only did the big rangy house offer the possibilities of subletting, but the big front window, bulging out into a bay, also afforded opportunities. The front room was large and clean. It wasn't a week until a carpenter had made yellow pine shelves and a counter, and delicious odors wafted from Mrs. Moore's kitchen. Then big trays of brown cookies and puffy cinnamon rolls, varnished with brown-sugar sirup, appeared in the window.

Lydia helped her. Finally she got to serving little lunches—easy-to-make sandwiches, hot drinks, pie, baked beans, and cottage cheese.

Shopgirls used to stop in and eat, for Mother Moore charged a reasonable price, and her helpings were big and generous. Shoppers with bulging bags would rest in one of her wooden chairs and order hot chocolate and baked beans and cheese sandwiches, crusty and hot.

Lydia waited on the tables, and in the lull between

meals washed great piles of dishes in a big pan of frothy suds.

One wild windy evening in late fall Lydia took a sudden notion to go to church. She tried to get her sister Kathleen to go with her, but she was stretched out in a Morris chair with an interesting book, and couldn't be prevailed upon to leave the house.

"No, no, no!" she yawned, never once looking up from her book. "Too cold and nasty out. No fit night to be out anyway." The windows were astream with water, and the wind blew in mournful little howls around the corners of the house. Lydia finally prevailed upon Chester, her younger brother, to go with her, on condition that she would make a platter of nut fudge afterwards. This she promised to do, and the two went out into the night.

"Where'll we go, sis?" asked her brother curiously. "Baptist, Methodist, 'Piscopalian?"

"Well, you see, it's this way, Chester. I saw a big sign up in front of Travers Hall announcing some kind of evangelistic meetings there. It sounded pretty interesting to me —all about prophecies in Daniel and Revelation, those queer beasts you read about, you know."

"Aw, sis, the preacher up at our church says no one no way can un'rstand them books. I ast him, I did," protested her little brother.

"Well, anyway, let's see; might be nothing to it. You can't tell. But I just wanted to see."

Then she lowered her big black umbrella and the two hurried into the commodious vestibule of Travers Hall. A good-sized crowd was assembling, and the back seats were already full. They had to take seats well up toward the front. Then they sat down and looked around. There were three chairs on the platform and a pulpit desk. An upright piano stood at one side. There was a buzz of conversation as the people came in, and quiet-voiced ushers courteously showed them to their places. Then the meeting began—such a meeting as Lydia had never before heard. It was all about the absolute surety of the coming of the Lord.

The minister, a tall man with his hair whitened at the temples, nailed every statement, every truth he presented, with a "Thus saith the Lord." The room was as still as death except for the emphatic voice of the preacher pointing out the milestones on the way to heaven. "Wars and rumors of wars," "false christs," "false prophets, famines, pestilences, perilous times, earthquakes, increase of knowledge." So surely and solidly were the evidences and certainties built up that when Lydia and Chester arose to go at the close of the meeting, she believed in the "second coming" with all her heart.

"Boy! That sure was one great sermon!" breathed Chester boyishly when they were out on the street again. Then he looked sidewise at his sister. "You don't hafta make me any candy fer goin'," he said, "'cause it was so good I'm goin' again."

"Well, I am too," answered Lydia. "But I'm going to make you some candy. I'm hungry for some myself."

Later in the evening, over a big platter of penuche fudge, full of nut meats and smooth as butter, the two agreed that they would keep their trip to themselves lest the others laugh at them.

"Mother would be sure to say they were fanatics," said Lydia, "but I never heard anything proved so absolutely."

"Me neither," answered Chester, his mouth full of fudge. "I like the feller too; he seems kinda different from most of 'em. He just gets down there and shakes hands as if he was really tickled to see you. I am sure goin' again."

That winter in Philadelphia, Lydia learned the real truths of the Bible. Every meeting they attended brought some new phase of truth to her notice that she had never known before, and it was hard for her not to tell her mother. Something kept her from doing so; possibly it was the devotion that her mother had ever had for the church of her girlhood. Every Sunday morning, rain or shine, cold or heat, would find her mother in her old black silk with its snowy collar, cuffs, and fichu. And she would be off to the "services" with as many of her children as she could prevail upon to go with her.

At last the day came when Lydia knew she must not work on the Sabbath any more. The knowledge lay upon her like a terrible weight.

Saturday was such a busy day at the bakery-restaurant. Lydia well knew that if she refrained from working, it would make it terribly hard for her mother, who was not young any more. The decision was a difficult one to make. There were literally hundreds of rolls to prepare out of the plump dough, raisins, cinnamon, and brown sugar. Great puffy loaves had to be removed from the ovens, oiled, and left on spotless bakery shelves to breathe their crusty fragrance to the hungry populace. Pies of every kind were achieved: raisin pies, bubbling black juice through the crust perforations; cherry, cloying in a thick bed of gelatinous juice; apple, succulent and inviting.

Lydia fell into a kind of terror. The day of God was drawing on apace. The signs were pointing irrefutably to that hour when all things would be dissolved. And here she was, chained by love to old ways not of the Lord.

Her gentle mother, always working too hard, did not dream of the agony her child was undergoing. She was too busy directing the cleaning woman, Anna, who, with mop bucket in hand, was always washing or mopping up something. Her hands were as hard as a pine board and shapeless from constant immersion in strong, hot water. Mrs. Moore hustled about doing the hundred and one tasks about the shop. She was vaguely worried a little about Lydia, who was always so different from the rest of her children—more inscrutable.

And then Friday came. All day Lydia worked breathlessly, as if by hurrying she might do two days' work in one. But it was like trying to mop up the sea. Her head was aching; her feet felt as if they were blazing when the sun dropped in the west. Her face must have told something of her misery, for her mother looked at her sharply when she came into the bakery for a moment.

"You are working too hard, Lydia; you are as pale as a ghost. Go to your room and don't get up, even tomorrow." Then raising her voice, she called to another daughter in the rear of the house. "Kathleen, get in here and tend the bakery. Lydia ain't a bit well and hasn't been for days."

Gratefully Lydia went to her room. She took off her old worn shoes and crept into her clean nightgown. Then her mother was there, turning down the bed and smoothing the pillow. She even had a flatiron, warm and wrapped in clean flannel, for Lydia to put her feet on. While she bustled about the room, she talked comfortingly to her child.

"I just saw all the time you were diggin' in and goin' at it too hot and heavy. There now, is that iron too hot to your feet? I had Anna leave them on the back of the range after she ironed today. Thought I'd take one to bed myself. Awfully chilly and damp out. Do you need another cover? I'll send Kathleen in with a glass of hot milk. Ain't nothin' better fer a person that's ailin' than somethin' hot." Turning down the lamp, she left the room in restful semidarkness.

Lydia, straight as a spar under the warm bedclothes, and trying to still her aching heart, was well on the way to a solution to her trouble, though she little knew it.

Then—it came over her that they could do without her. This was God's way of helping her to keep her first Sabbath when she was too weak and childlike to decide for herself. It was just at sunset that she had grown so sick. Why had that happened? Even now, remotely, she could hear the clatter of pans and the front door of the shop slam when a customer came in or went out. Savory odors that tantalized hungry, cold people left her unmoved. She was used to them.

Turning on her side, she brought the lamp nearer to the bed and turned the flame up. The pine shade threw a mellow glow across her pillow. She took her Bible and opened it, and began to read texts she had marked down from her attendance at the Adventist meetings. It was so beautiful and restful lying there and reading those verses that were as living water to her thirsty soul. "Ho, every one that thirsteth, come ye to the waters, and he that hath no money; come ye, buy, and eat; yea, come, buy wine and milk without money and without price."

The next morning her mother, busy and bustling, came into the room.

"Now, you just rest today, Lydia. That Kathleen has played 'grand lady' and let you do all the hard work long enough. From now on you can work at the housework and let her take over in the bakery. Why, I just found out today, not a lick of cleanin' has been done except what Anna does. Anna ain't got time to do all that, what with the washin' and ironin' and scrub work. Kathleen won't have time to lie around and read novels in the bakery. Now, you just rest up today, and you can be the housekeeper from now on. You'll do a good job of it, I know. And Miss Kathleen can just snap around and limber up her joints." Then she hurried out and left Lydia to rest. It was a beautiful day for her. All day she rested and read and kept her first Sabbath. When the sun went down that evening she got up and dressed and went into the big kitchen.

No one was there, for Saturday night was a rush time in the bakery. Anna had cleaned up after the noonday luncheon and had gone home. The dishpan was inverted on the table, and the ragged old gray dishcloth was spread out on top of it to dry. Lydia replenished the fire and put some bread in the oven to toast. Then she prepared a pot of delicious hot chocolate. Her mother loved it when she came in after the bakery was closed.

Lydia felt fresh and happy. If she just had the housework to do, most certainly she could arrange her affairs so that she could keep the Sabbath. Friday was the preparation day, the evangelist had said. She would prepare on that day. And Saturday morning she would go to church. No one need ever know. With the work she had now as her share, her religion would be easy to conceal.

But Lydia had not realized that a true child of God must not conceal the good news of salvation. She had not realized that the whole spread of the gospel message depends upon true Christians telling it again and again, gladly, gloriously, even in the face of disapproval and opposition.

Sunday night she took her umbrella and went to the meeting. Her face was wreathed in smiles. When the call came for those who would "give up all," Lydia was one of the first to spring to her feet. After the meeting she told the evangelist of her plans for keeping the Sabbath.

"And I won't need to tell a soul about it," she finished, her face flushing joyfully. But she was not quite prepared for the look of concern that spread over the evangelist's countenance.

"Why, are you ashamed of it?" he asked her quietly.

Lydia hesitated and looked up into his face, a little surprised at first, then condemned and somewhat bewildered.

The man continued to look down at her. Then he spoke again:

"Miss Moore, what of your people? Isn't this truth precious enough to you to make you want to share it with those you love? What would have happened if Peter or Paul or Matthew, Mark, Luke, or John had tried to hide the light? Where would we be tonight? Paul, who had known damp, dark prisons, who had been chained hand and foot, who had endured stoning and cursing, said, 'I am not ashamed of the gospel of Christ.'"

Tears filled Lydia's big brown eyes. Her lips trembled piteously like a child's.

"I—I—didn't mean to be ashamed," she faltered. "I ju—just thought they'd laugh at me and make fun."

The evangelist assured her of the stand she should take, and when she went out into the wind-swept April night she thought her heart would burst with joy. The streets were wet with rain and the wind was sharp, but Lydia saw none of it. She was breathless—eager to get home—to tell "the folks" the good news of salvation. Surely—they too would see it in all its beauty!

"While I am glad, Lydia," her mother remarked the next morning, "that you are trying to be a Christian, I don't see why you want to be such an odd one and choose such a crazy belief."

They were sitting at the breakfast table. Kathleen was caring for the bakery. From the big sunny kitchen they could hear the slam of the front door and the rattle of paper when Kathleen wrapped up buns, bread, or rolls.

Lydia was still pale and shaken from the scene of the evening before. Her sister had been loud in her jeering and laughter at Lydia's "new religion," as she had called it. Her mother had argued with her for hours, each determined to convince the other. Both of them were equally stubborn. They had to call a truce—for the hour had grown late. Both of them knew that the work of the morrow would call for their freshened strength.

Before going to bed, Lydia had read more from the writings of the apostle Paul. She read of another Lydia, a seller of purple, who had been converted by Paul in the ancient city of Philippi. She too was Lydia. She too had been converted to Jesus, the same Christ who led Paul all his wonderful life. That other Lydia sold purple, the richest and most beautiful color ever made by man, a color thought of in connection with gold and ermine and pearls and fine linen—a royal thing—purple, associated with emperors, kings, and princes. And then a sweet resolve came into Lydia's loving heart. She too would deal in precious things as did that other Lydia—things that pertained to the kingdom. She would deal in the royal things of God. And then she had gone to bed, to sleep sweetly and dreamlessly through the balmy spring night.

She had risen fresh and inspired to meet her perplexed loved ones at breakfast.

Her mother's pleasant round face was sober as she looked at her younger daughter. Lydia realized with sinking heart that her mother was resolved to overrule her beliefs that day and try to undo all she had learned. Only that morning she had read again from Paul: "For I am persuaded, that neither death, nor life, nor angels, nor principalities, nor powers, nor things present, nor things to come, nor height, nor depth, nor any other creature, shall be able to separate us from the love of God, which is in Christ Jesus our Lord." Lydia made a like resolve; her soft red lips grew firm with determination.

There on the corner of the table she saw a fat letter addressed to her old Quaker grandmother far up in the woods of northern Pennsylvania. She fairly trembled when she saw it. She knew then what her mother was up to. She was appealing to her grim, hardheaded old mother to straighten her daughter out. Her heart ached for her mother.

"Lydia," her mother said patiently, when the girl began to pick up the cups and plates after breakfast was over, "I want you to get your clothes packed. I am going to send you up to Mother's to spend a few weeks. You are to start a week from today, if that is all right with Mother."

She said nothing to her daughter about her purpose in sending her. But Lydia knew why. She knew that her mother hoped she would give up her belief in the newly found truth if she was taken away from the evangelistic meetings. She felt sad, but she knew that instead of forgetting, she would be strengthened. Neither life nor death, nor principalities nor powers, would separate her from the love of God.

That morning she hastened with her work. The great house was made immaculate by her skillful fingers. Never had she worked faster and harder. She must get all through so that after lunch she could go to Evangelist Martin's and tell him the turn her affairs had taken. So her scalloped potatoes, baked in the brown baking dish, were crusty and brown and ready to eat at high noon. She made muffins and boiled some eggs and shelled and put them in with a freshly opened can of tiny pickled beets. The eggs turned as red as the beets, and it made an inviting dish for the luncheon table.

During Kathleen's regime she had drawn upon the foods from the bakery for luncheon, and had set the table in her characteristic slapdash fashion. Who was hungry for baked beans after serving them to someone else all morning? or raisin cookies or cottage cheese? Therefore, Lydia's meal was doubly inviting, because it contained the element of surprise and was daintily and neatly served.

"I do declare, Lydia," her mother said as she collapsed into her chair, "I never saw anything that looked so good. Did you put onions in these potatoes? Good. And pickled eggs, a favorite of mine." She interrupted herself to stoop over pantingly and remove her great sprawling oxfords. "My feet ache like a toothache," she complained, not bitterly, but more to impart some casual information.

It did not take Lydia a half hour to set the kitchen in perfect order after the noon meal. Every crumb was carefully swept up and consigned to the great cookstove that Lydia kept polished and immaculate. The dishes were washed and carefully put away in the large cupboard, which Lydia had spent hours setting in order. Then she straightened the curtains, put a potted begonia in the middle of the table, and the room was done.

The Martins lived in an apartment on the second floor of a pleasant little row of brick store buildings about a twenty-minute walk from Lydia's home. She was very happy and very beautiful when she got there. Her cheeks were flushed and her lips were red from the exercise. Her tan hat and trim tan suit made her look very sweet indeed when she was admitted to the Martins' parlor.

The minister and his good wife soon saw that Lydia's people were going to leave no stone unturned to draw her away from her new allegiance. Their kind hearts were troubled for the girl. She saw it in their eyes.

"Oh, you do not need to worry!" she exclaimed, laughing at their sober faces. "I may be new in this message, but I have weighed it and proved it beyond every doubt, to my own satisfaction. I know it is the truth. And when I have convinced myself in this way, I am just as stubborn as Mother—or Grandma too, for that matter. But what I want is some books—you surely have some—so I can read on the train and be able to talk intelligently when I get up there. There is no use in my going if I can't speak up and defend myself. I want to know Daniel 2 and Daniel 7 well enough to tell it with at least a semblance of authority. I want Grandma to know this. She'll interpret stumbling and hesitation as weakness. I know her."

Pastor Martin's face cleared in relief. "I declare, young lady, you are going after this in the right way." He arose, went to his supply, and returned with a stack of books. Lydia looked at some of the titles interestedly—*Heralds of the Morning, Daniel and the Revelation, Our Paradise Home, Matthew Twenty-four.*

"Are these for sale, Pastor?" inquired Lydia. "I want to buy them so I can use them."

So Lydia bought the books and carried them home in an old-fashioned telescope suitcase that Mrs. Martin gave her. That night she began to study as she had never studied before in her life. She had the Daniel part of *Daniel and the Revelation* read through by the end of the week, and had a tiny notebook full of neat, concise notes. Lydia was determined to know whereof she spoke.

So the next Monday Lydia, with her valise and telescope suitcase, was sent north to unlearn the ways of the kingdom. It was her first missionary journey. Like Paul of old, she set out toward her Ephesus, her Antioch, her Philippi, with a prayer on her lips, a song in her heart, and armed with the sword of the Spirit—and with her purple of the kingdom to sell as did that other Lydia.

For a while Lydia curiously watched the landscape as it whisked by, for she had not traveled much, and it was a great novelty to her. Lush pastures with cattle knee-deep in grass; big, trim farmhouses; brown roads and trickling brooks interested her for a time. Then, realizing that she must prepare her "purple"—her royal wares of the kingdom—she unstrapped the funny little telescope suitcase and drew out *Matthew Twenty-four,* a thin little blue book, and began to read.

"Oh, it is wonderful, it is precious," she thought as she read. "How truly and surely the Lord has even put His finger on the very generation that will see Him come!" It thrilled Lydia immeasurably to know that she was living in that "grand and awful time." History had truly been pouring into the very mold of prophecy. O that God would give her fluency and wisdom and knowledge to present this wonderful truth to those who were going to question it! And Lydia, the seller of twentieth-century purple of the kingdom, prayed to the God of that other Lydia for the diplomacy, the wisdom, and the salesmanship that she knew she would sorely need very soon.

The spring day had been warm and bright. Lydia had been so absorbed in her reading that before she realized it she was very hungry. She laid the book face down on the dull, dusty plush of the seat opposite her and got out the lunch her mother had prepared. It was put up neatly and tastefully in a small cardboard box. There was a small bag of cookies, crunchy with nuts and rich with raisins. Her mother had peeled an orange and wrapped it in paper. There were egg sandwiches and delicious lettuce-and-cottage-cheese sandwiches.

Almost before she knew it, the brakeman called out the name of the tiny town where her grandmother lived, and she was scrambling off with her valise and the old telescope suitcase of books.

Her grandmother's hired man was at the station to meet her in his old spring wagon. Lydia had known him since she was a little child.

"Hello, Hank!" she called. The lean, bewhiskered old fellow darted a look in her direction, then, smiles wreathing his grizzled old face, he ran across the splintered platform to meet her.

"Why, Lyddy!" he shrilled in his high old squeaky voice. "Ain't you growed! I wouldn't 'a' knowed you!"

Seizing her luggage, he led the way to the wagon, put it in the back, and told her to climb in and wait for him.

"Got a little tradin' t' do fer yer granny at the gen'l store. She ain't able t' make the trip much any more, and I fetch in her eggs and butter, and do her tradin' fer her."

Lydia climbed over the wheel and surveyed the tiny village of Hooperville. Just a ramshackle row of stores and a few houses clustered nearby.

She saw old Hank shambling down the dusty road toward the stores, with a basket on each arm. She knew that in one were the neat pats of butter stamped with the old wooden mold that made a sculptured acorn on the top. In the other were the big, brown, fresh eggs.

Lydia smiled a little to herself, though not humorously, at the real reason why she was here and at the utter futility of it all.

"Nor life, nor death, nor any other creature shall be able to separate me," she murmured. Just then old Hank came shambling back, both his baskets full of bags, packages, and cans. He climbed clumsily up to the seat beside her and clucked to the bony old horse, who paid no heed whatever to him but stood patiently switching her sparse tail apathetically. Hank seized his stubby whip and nipped the old equine gently on her flanks. She gave a nervous leap and started out with a great show of speed, almost knocking Lydia off the seat, but slowed down almost immediately to a snail's pace.

In due time the sight of her grandmother's old house met her eyes. Squat, low, weathertight, it gave the impression that it was a living creature. The two front windows were eyes and the great front door was the mouth. It looked watchfully out upon the smooth lawn bordered with old-fashioned flowers.

As Hank's squeaking old vehicle drew near, Lydia saw

that her grandmother was out in the front yard. There was a table out there and Lydia could see she was working with ever so many little packets of seeds.

Alighting from the old wagon, Lydia hastened across the lawn toward her grandmother. Hank toiled pantingly behind with her luggage.

Calmly, by way of greeting, the old woman extended a great tin dipper to the girl.

"Thee is thirsty," she said in her mellow, solicitous voice. "The trip is dusty and long."

Lydia, knowing her grandmother, took the dipper, went to the pump, and drank deeply of the clear, cold water. The old woman went right on sorting her seeds, as if Lydia's coming were an everyday occurrence.

When the girl came back to the table, she said to her, "Thee is hungry, too. Get thee something to eat."

And Lydia went into the big kitchen. From a stone crock, back in one corner by a worktable, she took a great loaf of brown, homemade bread. Cutting off a slice, she got a spoon, a glass, and a knife from an old cupboard with perforated tin doors. The cellar, entered from the back hallway, was a deep, cool room, floored with flagstones. In one corner was a large flat cooler filled with spring water that entered from one end and trickled out the other. It made a tiny lake in the field beyond.

Lydia took a plate from a low crock and spread her bread with some butter from the big slab her grandmother had saved for family use. Then she took a dipper, and pushing back the heavy cream from the top of the tall milk crock, she filled her glass. Never had anything tasted better. She drank two glasses, ate her bread, and then went up into the yard with her grandmother.

The little old woman was bent, her thinning gray hair scarcely covering the pink flesh of her scalp. Her face was autographed with the puzzles, the worries, the sorrows, and the sufferings of time. But she was young in spirit. She looked up when Lydia came back to the table.

"Thee has a new religion, Lydia," she stated without ceremony.

"Yes, Grandma," Lydia smiled. "Mother sent me up here to get you to 'straighten me out,' but, Grandma, I told her it would be no use. What I have found is truth, and I won't be separated from it."

"Of course thee won't," agreed her grandmother wisely. "If thee is right, thee is too much like me to be willy-nilly. If thee is right thee would die for thy religion."

Quite suddenly Lydia loved the old woman with a love she had never before realized.

"Thee must wash and rest," she went on kindly. "In the morning thee must tell me all about it."

The room that she occupied at her grandmother's house was spacious and clean. The old walnut bureau, with its two tiny drawers jutting up on the top like high shoulders, occupied a prominent place in the room. The curtains were snowy white and starched stiff. They lifted and swayed in the breeze. Lydia lay straight under the white spread and looked up into the velvet darkness. It seemed a friendly night, with all the little creatures holding some kind of "hosanna" meeting out in the long grasses of the meadow.

She turned her head and looked through the open window into the firmament studded with stars. It seemed almost as if she could reach out and pick them like daisies. Then the thought occurred to her that somewhere among the starlit aisles of glory was the home of the Lord, and the throne of His Father. The thought was wonderfully comforting to the girl as she lay there that sweet summer night.

The next morning the aroma of breakfast came up to meet her. It was broad daylight, and from the window she could see Hank driving the team out of the gate, bound for one of Grandma's distant fields. Hurriedly she washed her face at the washstand and dried it on one of Grandma's snowy huckaback towels. Then, dressed in a clean work dress, she hurried downstairs.

The table was set. After turning the toast in the oven, Grandma greeted the girl. Then pulling the frying pan over to the hot part of the stove, she broke two eggs into it.

"Come, get thee and me a bowlful of cereal, Lydia," her grandmother said kindly, "and take out the toast. Thee don't eat pork, so I am cooking eggs."

Lydia knew by that that her grandmother had certainly been well informed as to her religious beliefs.

After breakfast she washed the dishes and cleaned the kitchen. When she got through, she discovered her grandmother in the sunny front room, sitting with a huge basket of mending by her side. She motioned the girl to a chair beside her.

"Get thy Bible, child, and tell me all about it," the old woman said kindly. "I won't promise thee that I will believe, but I will hear thee through. If thee has error, I will tell thee and help thee. If thee has truth, thee can help me."

Lydia ran up the old stairs and gladly brought down the telescope case full of books. She took it into the room where her grandmother was. Together they sat down at a fine old mahogany table.

Then Lydia, with the straightforward simplicity of a

child, began to tell her story—to sell her purple of the kingdom. Through Daniel 2, Daniel 7, and Daniel 8 and 9, she went surely, remembering every explanation of the truth, and treasuring it as if it had been pearls and rubies and fine purple such as that other Lydia sold.

The old clock in the corner ticked knowingly, as if he were whispering to himself with his hands in front of his face about the strange goings on in the room. The sun grew blood red and began to slip behind the rim of the world.

Suddenly the old woman rose, tut-tutted loudly, and peered at the clock in the half darkness.

"Thee has such an interesting story, Lydia, that I clean forgot all about supper. That Hank will have two hollow legs this night. He has been planting and plowing all day. Thee help me with supper and then tell me more in the morning."

The old woman shook the woodstove noisily and put in some corncobs. The fire roared up the pipe. Lydia sliced some cold boiled potatoes into a hot skillet with minced onion and melted butter, and set it to frying on the back lid. The old woman mixed up biscuits and cut them into thick, smooth disks on the floury board, her wrinkled hands working swiftly and surely. Lydia opened a can of tomatoes and added butter and little squares of toast. And then the old woman cleaned a dishful of long green onions to be eaten with hot biscuits and fresh butter.

When Hank lumbered onto the back porch and began his noisy ablutions at the washbasin and roller towel, the biscuits were a golden brown, puffy and light, and the sour-cream gravy Lydia had made was ready to pour into the bowl.

"Lydia," her grandmother laughed, as she shut the drafts on the stove, "I never got such a quick supper before in my whole life. With thee to help me, we could start one of those quick lunchrooms people like so much." Then laughing, all of them, they sat down to eat.

Lydia had never seen her grandmother rush things through so quickly as she did the next morning. She was even up a half hour earlier, setting her bread, putting beans to soak, and peeling potatoes, so that they could study with fewer interruptions. When Lydia got through with the dishes, she saw that her grandmother even had the books laid out on the table. She was sitting there leafing through them, fairly quivering with eagerness. Her back was bowed by the burdens of years. Her old black sprigged calico was clean and ironed smooth. She wore a white apron edged with knitted lace, as usual.

"Come on, Lydia; I'm fairly atremble to hear what thee has to say. I tell thee, child, I have heard more Bible from thee than I've heard in forty years from that pastor of ours. Thee has showed me things I didn't know were in the good old Book."

Then, with fearful joy and many an upward lift of her heart to God, Lydia began to tell the old woman of the Sabbath. First she cited all the Biblical authority she could find from the texts given her at the evangelistic meetings. Then she got more from her copy of *Bible Readings*. From here, she swung into the change of the Sabbath as predicted in Daniel 7:25 and corroborated so exactly in history.

"And so, Granny dear, they changed it, just to accommodate their heathen leanings. And they brag about it. I wouldn't think so much of it if it hadn't been written of in the Good Book."

The old woman had said not a word all the time. She looked up Bible verses and seemed to hang on every word her granddaughter said. Her bright brown eyes did not miss a thing. When Lydia hesitated a moment, the old woman, looking at the clock, rose with alacrity, and went to her room to dress. She had a plan in mind, but said nothing to Lydia about it.

Leaving the house, she had Hank take her in the buggy to see her pastor, determined to check with him and find out the truth. Her visit with the minister was very unsatisfactory; he could prove nothing contrary to the statements that Lydia had made, especially regarding the Sabbath. In fact, the interview was so disconcerting to the grandmother that she left in a hurry. She then thought of securing the schoolhouse for lectures, and determined that Lydia should preach there.

Grandma Wright spent the next two hours visiting one member of the school board after another. They were amused and curious at her request. All of them gave their laughing consent. Grandma Wright's granddaughter, a girl of twenty, was going to preach. What a laugh! Well, there'd be a crowd. The whole town would turn out for that. What Lydia would have to say to these arrangements, Granny didn't even care. Anyone who could talk and explain things so well to one person surely ought to be able to do it for a hundred or even two hundred. She engaged the schoolhouse for four weeks of evening meetings, beginning the very next Sunday night. No need to do much advertising. The news went through the town like wildfire. Then she trotted happily home to tell Lydia the good news.

Dinner was all over when she finally got back. Lydia was washing up the dishes, and Hank had gone back to the field. Granny sat down at the table eagerly. She loved good food, and Lydia was a good cook. She had eaten her creamed potatoes and johnnycake—yellow as butter—and was beginning on her apple pie when she broke the news to Lydia. It struck the girl like a thunderbolt. She was speechless, and stared at the old woman as if she had taken leave of her senses.

"Wh-wh-why, Granny!" she gasped. "I can't preach. Why, I don't know enough about the Bible to speak in front of a crowd! Why, why, why, I'd be scared to death!"

But this declaration on Lydia's part did not affect the old woman's composure in the least. She went right on eating her pie and finished with a wedge of cheese.

"That was fine pie, Lyddy. Did thee use those apples in the south bin? Good. Thee did right. They are the best. Thee has three days to get ready for the first meeting, my girl. Take thy books and go up and study. I shall do all the work. Anyway, thee shan't be bothered. Tomorrow is, as thee has said, the preparation day. Thee shall see how I shall prepare for the Sabbath. Thee and me, we shall keep it together."

Lydia kissed the old woman tenderly, and both their faces—Lydia's smooth young one and Grandma's old wrinkled one—were wet with tears. Then Lydia gathered up her books, some paper, and some sharpened pencils, and went upstairs. She dared not fail Granny now. The God in heaven who had helped Saul of Tarsus would not fail her in her hour of great need.

She knelt by the bed to pray, and there poured out her soul to the Source of all wisdom and understanding. And when at last she arose, it was with a feeling of confidence born of a precious faith in the Lord.

Grandma Wright then called Hank in and had him hitch up the old bay mare. As soon as she had done the dishes she set out to inform the neighborhood. They all liked Granny, and everyone promised to be on hand to hear Lydia's message.

"Why, sure, Grandma. We'll be there. What time Sunday night? Seven-thirty? Fine. Betcha that room will be jammed to the doors. Is that Hattie's youngest girl? Funny she'd take up preachin'. But then they say that girls can preach as good as men, once they take a notion."

From farmhouse to farmhouse she went, her old face fairly glowing with altruism. Deep down in her heart she was pardonably proud of Lydia and deeply disgusted with the preacher. She had hoped, yes, expected, that he would have some kind of refutation or explanation ready for her when she asked him about the Sabbath. But, no. All he did was to get mad, and that was the first time she had ever gone to him for any kind of spiritual help. After all these years—and this was the kind of answer she got! Her Lydia would be able to tell the people the truth, since he hadn't.

Then she drove over to the schoolhouse. She had obtained the key, for she wanted to go in and look things over. The room would have to be cleaned well before the meeting. She couldn't abide dirt. School had been dismissed for the summer, and over the whole room hung an odor reminiscent of chalk dust, stale lunches, and mice. The windows were dirty; the floors were grimy; the blackboards were smeared. Some child had left an old sweater sagging on a nail in the cloakroom, and another had left a lunch pail sprawling open, the dried crusts of bread spilled out on the floor.

The old woman sniffed; then she went out and locked

the door. To a tiny cottage across the road she bent her footsteps. Two or three little children were playing in the front yard, and a snowy wash billowed on the clothesline.

"Hello, Huldy," she said to the pleasant-faced woman who appeared at the door. "My granddaughter Lydia is going to have meetings in the schoolhouse. I know thee likes to earn a little money once in a while. I am willing to pay thee well to scour and clean it. Thee will do it well. Does thee want the job?"

The woman's face broke into a smile. "Why, yes, Grandma, I'll be glad to earn a little money just now. Interest is comin' due on that mortgage, and we want to make a good payment on the principal this time. We want to pay them all we can rake and scrape together."

"Then, thee clean it tomorrow, Huldy. Mind, I don't want thee finishing on Saturday. I will send Hank tomorrow afternoon with the money. I must get home and get supper now. Lyddy is studying for her sermons."

But when she got home, Lydia had supper almost ready. She had gone through her notes of the first evangelistic meeting she had attended, and had looked up all she could find from *Bible Readings, Heralds of the Morning,* and *Matthew Twenty-four.* Her mind was so tired after five hours of hard mental work that it was a relaxation for her to get supper. She was ladling steaming soup into bowls when her grandmother came in, tired and hungry.

"Thee doesn't know how good that smells, Lyddy. I hadn't aimed for thee to get supper, but I am glad thee did. I get tired of my own concoctions and like to taste someone else's cookin'."

When Lydia arrived at the schoolhouse on that bright May night it was already full to overflowing. Horses and rigs of every type were in the yard, and as it was a mild night, all the windows were open. Her heart plunged in terror at first. Then the thought came to her that there would stand beside her this night the same Person who stood by that other Lydia back in ancient Thyatira, where she sold her purple. The same One who stood by Paul.

Perhaps they, too, were terrified at first, and with good reason. Many of them were persecuted and martyred for preaching Christ. Paul must have felt so when he said, "Yet not I, but Christ liveth in me." A sweet peace and serenity stole over her. Quite suddenly she was not afraid. When she came in she looked absolutely calm.

One of the members of the school board had yielded to Granny's solicitations and led a song service before the meeting. "Old Hundred," "How Firm a Foundation," and even "America" wafted out on the gentle breeze. Then Gramp Hewitt prayed, his knotted old hands trembling, clasping the top of his cane. The hour had come.

Lydia arose and laid her Bible on the desk. As one who was inspired, she told the story of the coming of the Lord, sweetly and clearly, reading the corroborating Bible verses. The room was soundless; not even the shuffling of feet or sideways whispers disturbed the breathless quiet.

The whole roomful of people bent forward to catch every word. A few had papers or old envelopes and were jotting down texts. The hour of service seemed very short—it was also interesting and strange and wonderful. Then when Lydia, in a gentle voice, invited them to come again on Tuesday night, saying she would explain the prophecy of Daniel 2, a buzz of interest went through the room. They wouldn't miss that. No sirree. Grandma Wright's girl sure knew her Bible.

And the crowd scattered, filled with anticipation for the meetings that were to follow.

Lydia went on through four weeks of meetings, four evenings a week—even marveling at herself, but well knowing the Source of her strength. Every night the little red brick structure was crowded to the doors. Some of the young bloods even built trestles so that they could stand at the windows. Every window was full of heads. It might have been disconcerting to Lydia a year before, but not now. Each day found her calmer and more composed. The hours of study that she well knew were absolutely essential for her talks opened up even more of the blessed truth to her. She truly rejoiced with those she taught in the new things she found in her *Bible Readings*.

Granny would shake her head many times in the days to come as she went about her work. One day Lydia, from her upstairs room, saw the old woman emerge from the tool shed with a spade. Wondering, she leaned out of the window to watch her. What in the world was Granny doing with a spade? Hank did all the digging and gardening and farming, and was positively jealous of his work.

The old woman made for the herb bed just south of the farmhouse. Here grew sage, thyme, and summer savory besides some medicinal plants she had dug up in the woods and domesticated for fever, ague, and other ills peculiar to human beings. She began to dig in the mealy soil between the rows. Lydia was amazed at the progress she made. At first she thought to call out that she would help her. Then it occurred to her that perhaps Granny too, like Hank, wanted to be "let alone."

The very bend of her back indicated she was up to something important. It wasn't long till she had a sizable hole dug, and a big heap of earth was piled up at one side. She then trotted off out of sight behind the house.

Lydia hadn't long to wait before the old woman hove into view again, bowed over with the load she was carrying. What was it she had? Lydia parted the curtains and leaned out to look. Why, it was hams and bacon and jowls that Grandma had smoked over hickory with such arduous toil last fall. Lydia remembered the great box of them that had come to her home by express from Grandma. Tears glistened in the girl's eyes. Oh, it was wonderful, wonderful to be a "seller of purple," to publish the good news of salvation, to see the change the Word of God makes in the lives of men and women.

She watched the old woman throw the smoked swine's flesh into the hole, rake the dirt back into it, and tramp it down decisively. Then, rubbing her hands together as if to clear them from uncleanness, she picked up her tools and went to put them away. Well, Granny was all right. She was, indeed. No halfway work about her.

It was fortunate for Lydia that she had taken copious notes on the evangelistic meetings the past winter. It gave her a cue as to the sequence of the subjects—"The Coming of Christ," "Daniel 2," "Where Are the Dead?" "Where Is Hell?" "Where Is Heaven?" Then she filled in with other important subjects as the evangelist did, ending by emphasizing the perpetuity of the law, and the necessity of keeping the Christian Sabbath.

When she drew near the culmination of her time at the schoolhouse, Lydia wrote a long letter to her friend the evangelist back in Philadelphia and asked for help. She told him all about the interest, and ended by telling of the crowds.

Of course, the schoolhouse isn't large, but Granny counts 150 to 200 a night. She counts them as they go out the door. I know there will be a group of Sabbathkeepers, if someone is here to finish it right. So please come. Remember, even I haven't been baptized, and I feel just like a little child. So do come and help me. You can stay at Granny's house; she has said that I may invite you."

And so it came about that on the very last week of the meetings Lydia's friends, the evangelist and his wife, came up to help her. They carried Granny's reed organ over, and Mrs. Martin played for the singing. Sometimes Elder Martin sang something special, for he was the possessor of a fine, clear tenor voice. The town was truly turned upside down. On the last Friday, Granny, Lydia, and the preacher's wife were busy all day explaining how to get ready for the Sabbath. Nothing gave Granny more pleasure.

"Why, thee cleans the house and thee cooks and bakes as thee did when thee prepared for Sunday, only more. Thee saves thyself on the Sabbath more than thee did on Sunday. No cooking at all, Lyddy says. Only warmin' up. I cook potatoes with the jackets on and bake a pan of beans. Then a big cake and a pie of some kind. And that with my canned fruits and vegetables gives aplenty to eat without standin' over the cookstove all day. Thee knows well that Sunday was not a day of rest."

"No, I should say not," was the sympathetic rejoinder. "Why, with company comin' and goin' and Pa wantin' a big dinner with all the fixin's, it was the hardest day of the week for me."

"Thee can see," Granny replied sagely, "that the good Lord did not intend for thee to work full seven days a week. The Sabbath will be a blessing to thee and for this town. I told Sam Watson that Lyddy would turn this town upside down, and she has too."

That Friday night the Sabbath was observed in fifteen homes in that little village. Elder Martin spoke that night at the schoolhouse on the beauties of the new earth, and told them that the Sabbath would be kept there too. " 'From one new moon to another,' " he quoted, " 'and from one sabbath to another, shall all flesh come to worship before me, saith the Lord.'

"The observance of any other day is not even logical," he observed. "It would be silly for God to tell us to observe the Sabbath throughout our generations and then change it to Sunday, only to change it back to the Sabbath again in the new earth. We know that He did not do that. He said, 'I am the Lord, I change not.' It is when man goes off on ways of his own, and begins to do things that are wrong, that something changes. It is not God but man in his sin who separates himself from Him."

When Elder and Mrs. Martin told Lydia about college, she was eager to go. Just to think of being in a great group of young people, all of whom were interested in working for God! But there were the finances. Lydia knew that her mother would not help. She would be furious at this change in affairs anyway. Kind as her mother was, Lydia knew her to be capable of deep animosity. She would be prejudiced against anyone or anything that had contributed to the present state of affairs. Therefore, the girl knew that no help would be forthcoming from that quarter. As for Granny, Lydia knew that she had little money beyond her own small needs. If she, Lydia, got to go to school, it would have to be through her own resources. But her heart was light and her faith was strong.

The members of the infant church she had helped to raise up gave her a little party at the last. There was a whole suitcaseful of gifts they had brought to her. There were handkerchiefs, dresser scarfs, doilies, and stationery. Down at the bottom of the great pile of packages was a tiny flat package. Lydia opened it last. It was Granny's tiny gold Elgin watch. Lydia had often admired it in the old-fashioned jewel case with its padded satin lining. And now —it was her own. When she opened the package, Granny was by her side, watching her—alert as a little wren. There it lay in its satin bed, its engraved hunting case gleaming up at her like a shining eye. Tears sprang to Lydia's eyes, and she put both arms around the old woman and kissed her tenderly.

That night, down at the sleepy little station, Lydia boarded the train to go to college. The gaslights had been turned down in the waiting room where Hank, Lydia, and her grandmother waited. Presently, even before they heard the whistle, they felt the vibrations of the approaching train. Hank seized Lydia's bags and took them out on the platform. Swiftly, good-bys were murmured, and Lydia found herself aboard, straining her eyes to see her grandmother peering up through the darkness as the train moved off.

At first Lydia had been eager and sure of herself. Somewhere in that great college city there must be a place for her to earn and learn. She had had a childlike trust in God and an implicit faith that there would somehow be a solution. Now—with the bridges burned behind her, with the train roaring into the unknown, and with only a limp, worn five-dollar bill in her purse—Lydia became suddenly afraid. This was a presumptuous, daring thing to do. Why, if she failed, her mother back in Philadelphia would be ready with an "I told you so." It seemed that she could not bear to face life if that terrible thing became a reality. Then—then a sweet resolve came over her. Why, she need not fail. There was a promise somewhere—Paul had said it—maybe he had even said it to that other Lydia when she was discouraged, "I can do all things through Christ which strengtheneth me."

The first thing Lydia did when she arrived in the city where the college was situated was to purchase a morning paper. She sat down in the waiting room and scanned the "Help Wanted" columns. She had several weeks to work before school began in the fall, and then she could work half days. She checked her suitcase and went out to interview possible employers.

It was a weary, disheartening day. Some women were cold and calculating, determined to exact the last ounce of their pound of flesh for a miserable wage. Other places were out of the question. She bought a chocolate bar and a malted milk and then went on to complete her list.

It was late in the evening when she came to Ma Grant's boardinghouse. The window shades were up, and the house was full of a merry clatter. Indeed, her timid knock was not even heard. She walked to the kitchen door, which opened onto a big porch. All around the porch someone had painstakingly strung twine, and morning-glories had climbed them luxuriantly. An old cat sat at the screen door, peering in longingly. When Lydia knocked there was a sudden hush in the merry babble in the big kitchen. A large, fat woman of florid countenance was frying some kind of meat at a great black range.

"Sadie, you go to the door," she directed in a high

clear voice. "Somebody's knockin', and I can't leave this meat."

A tall, thin girl entered from the dining room and came to the door. She had flaxen hair braided and bound coronet fashion about her head. A huge black-and-white dog rushed growling to the door.

"Down, Roxie!" she called to the dog. "Be still and go back and lie down. Yes?" she added sweetly, speaking to Lydia.

"Did you—I mean—have you advertised for help? I —I——" But Sadie was opening the screen.

"Yes, we did," she said, "but you'll have to see Mother. She's the one who wants to talk to you. She's the one you'll have to work for." Then Lydia found herself looking into the face of a kind, motherly woman. She seemed to think the meat was done, for she forked the rest of it out of the skillet onto a meat platter up in the warming closet. Then she spooned some flour from a crock on the reservoir into the hot fat, and began stirring it, all the while keeping up a constant run of conversation.

"Sadie, fill them soup bowls. Boarders will be down in a minute. Have you had experience in a boardinghouse, dearie? A bakery and lunchroom? Well, that helps. I'll need you for just everything. Cleaning, baking, and cooking. Just helping with what there is to do. You can have one day off a week. Saturday? Why, that suits me fine. I'll let you run to town, too, sometimes to shop, if your work is done."

Lydia took the job. They wouldn't let her work that night, and one of the boarders, Cliff by name, was dispatched after her suitcase. Mrs. Grant had Sadie show her to her room.

It was on the third floor and was somewhat cramped, but it was clean. The roof sloped, and there was a wide dormer with double windows. Under a shelf in one corner new cretonne curtained off space for her clothes. There was a neat, narrow bed, with a strip of carpet in front of it, and a dresser with a wavy mirror. The other girls' rooms were on this floor, too, and Lydia knew she was going to like it. She was glad she could have the Sabbath off. That night she crept between coarse, clean sheets, singularly content. She had set a battered tin alarm clock for five o'clock. One of her duties was to help get breakfast. Later, the whole meal was to be her responsibility. Next Sabbath she would go over to the college and look things over. In just eight more weeks she would begin her beloved classwork. With a sigh of contentment she drifted off to sleep.

Lydia saved nearly every penny of her wages toward her college work. She knew there would be anxious days ahead that would try her very soul. Granny had told her she would help all she could, but the girl knew that would not be much. The old woman had very little money. The change from her five-dollar bill kept her in stamps and incidentals. Lydia thought of the barrel of meal and the cruse of oil one day, when her five dollars was almost gone. She had had to buy some gloves and hose downtown, and when she went home she found a visitor in the parlor with Mrs. Grant.

"Lydia," Mrs. Grant addressed her, "this is Mrs. Taylor. She is having a dinner party tonight and needs someone to help cook and serve. I told her you could go. I was just tellin' Sadie that when you get breakfast and dinner, I ain't going to work a free horse to death. You can earn a little extra money servin' or settin' up with children."

Lydia gratefully accepted her employer's kindness and went to serve for Mrs. Taylor that afternoon. She found Mrs. Taylor to be one of those nervous women who go to pieces under any added responsibility. The kitchen was a roomy, sunny place, but it looked as though a cyclone had gone through it. Neither the breakfast nor the dinner dishes were washed and everything was in a muddle. It was three o'clock, and the guests were to come at seven.

"If you'll give me your menu, Mrs. Taylor," she said, "I can get some of the harder things started; then I can clean up the kitchen."

But Mrs. Taylor had made no particular plans and so stated. She told Lydia to just go ahead, and she airily showed her where a few things were, gave her the grocer's telephone number, and walked out.

"I am due at the hairdresser's in ten minutes," she had said. "So just go right ahead and do as you please. Mrs. Grant said you were perfectly capable."

The first thing the girl did was to look over everything to see just what the woman had on hand. Lydia knew that by combining several of the odds and ends she found in the icebox, she could make a good clear soup. She would have mashed potatoes, gravy, dainty fluffy biscuits, and new peas. She found a bag of fresh peas in the entry and decided to hull them first. Then she'd wash the potatoes, so they would be ready to peel. And then she'd clean this horrid kitchen. It took her a full twenty minutes to shell the peas and wash the potatoes. Then she set a dishpan full of water on the gas stove to heat. But oh! The stove was so dirty that it was repulsive. She'd just have to scrub that stove, too! Then she began to assemble dishes. There were dirty dishes everywhere. She hurried as fast as she could, but in spite of all she could do, it was four-thirty before the dishes were all clean and shining on the table. Now to put them away. But one glance at the cupboards revolted the girl's orderly soul. She stood on a chair and organized and rearranged for another ten minutes. In another half hour dinner was well on the way, and the kitchen was in gleaming order, with the exception of the floor. It sadly needed wiping up, but Lydia knew she must direct her attention to the dining room and clean it while she watched her cake in the oven. The buffet was loaded down with hats, books, papers, old letters, needles, thread, and even a cake plate with a shriveled, dry baker's cake on it.

Lydia cleared them away and put them in their proper places as well as she knew. Then she cleaned the whole room thoroughly and polished the furniture and the woodwork. Next she searched through the buffet drawers for a tablecloth. There was not one there! Then the girl remembered a basketful of unironed clothes down in the basement by the ironing board! Could it be in that? Well, there was no time to speculate. If it must be done, it must be done.

Lydia took her cake out of the oven and left it to cool, then ran to the basement. Yes, there was the tablecloth, dampened and rolled up. Luckily the irons were hot. Mrs. Taylor had evidently built a fire in the old range with a view to heating her irons. (That was back before the days of electric irons, so poor Lydia had to fly like the wind.)

Mrs. Taylor was just coming in from town when Lydia came up the basement steps with the tablecloth and napkins, ironed satin smooth. Mrs. Taylor's hair had been done in elaborate rolls and puffs in the mode of the day. She looked into the kitchen a moment, then called, "I hope you will get the floor wiped up before tonight. My cook took 'French leave' a week ago, and it hasn't been washed since. I see you have cleaned the dining room. Well, I'll go up and lay out my things. Straighten up the parlor and my bedroom a little, if you get a chance, will you?" and she swept up the stairs.

Lydia felt a little resentful at her giving no word of commendation for all the work she had done, but she said not a word. Somehow she got it all done, and she was terribly tired.

When the guests arose from the beautifully appointed table to go into the parlor, Mr. Taylor stepped into the kitchen for a moment. He was bald and fat, and Lydia knew from all hearsay that he was fearfully henpecked.

"Just a little token of my appreciation for the splendid dinner," he said pompously. "Now this is in addition to what Mrs. Taylor will give you, so you'll please not mention it to her"—he looked about a little fearfully—"but I like to show my appreciation, too." And he gave her a two-dollar bill.

Later, when the dishes were all washed and the kitchen and dining room were in shining order, Mrs. Taylor bustled in. She gave Lydia a silver dollar and a quarter. "You have done very well for a beginner, Lydia," she said patronizingly, as if she feared that a little praise might do the girl actual harm. "I'll probably have you again if I don't get a regular girl."

Though such work was hard and rather aggravating, Lydia was pleased to get it occasionally. Her little bank account was steadily growing as the time drew near for school to begin. Granny sent her two dollars once and said she had had a good "combing" from Lydia's mother.

"Thee would think," the letter read, "that I had led thee into some kind of malicious mischief, the way Sarah acts. She says she will see thee dead before she helps thee in thy college course."

When school began, Lydia worked only half days at Mrs. Grant's, earning just barely enough to meet her expenses at school. Occasionally, on a Saturday night or a Sunday afternoon, she supplemented her "barrel of meal" and "cruse of oil" by some special employment Mrs. Grant would help her secure. The girl noticed time and again that she was never quite penniless. One Sunday afternoon she was helping a well-to-do Welsh woman on the edge of the city to engineer a particularly brilliant dinner. The woman was very irritable and dictatorial, and Lydia felt like screaming. But knowing that silence would be the best escape, she worked on faithfully and well. God seemed to reward the work of her hands. Everything she made was done beautifully and to a "turn." Suddenly the woman stopped in the kitchen door and said, "Come upstairs with me, Lydia. It won't take a minute."

Once they were in the beautiful bedroom, the woman began piling dresses on the bed, talking all the while.

"You're the nicest girl I ever had in my house. Most of them talk back and act smart with me. Well, I have more clothes than I can wear. You're working your way through school, and you can use these, I know. What size shoes do you wear? Well, I do, too. Don't worry. My husband buys me more than I can wear. I like you and I want to help you."

Lydia had to be taken home in a carriage that night so she could take all her treasures home. There were dresses for every occasion, a kimono, flounced and embroidered petticoats, and a full dozen pairs of shoes, hardly worn. There was a cloth coat with fur collar and cuffs and a warm inner lining. Besides that there was a two-dollar bill folded in her purse. Lydia felt that God had truly blessed her.

And so by virtue of the manifold ways that the good Lord has of helping His dear children, the girl got through the Bible instructor's course at college. But no call came for her right away. It seemed that she could not bear to go on working for the Grants when she did so yearn to be out in active work for the Lord. But the trial was good for her. She prayed harder; she worked harder.

One Sabbath at the college church an appeal was made for a Bible instructor to take over a group of people who had become interested through a colporteur's visit. There would be no money in it for anyone—not even carfare. Lydia accepted. She rode clear across the city every night, reading with one or another of the group. She grew deeply interested. It was her life—that she knew.

Before the summer was over Lydia had the joy of seeing two of these people baptized.

Then another experience came to her before she received the call for which she was praying. One of the workers in the bindery at the school had a very sick wife. People said she would die, and they could not afford to hire help. Neighbors just dropped in and helped and took turns, but things were in a sad state for the afflicted family. Lydia quit her job at the Grants and went to do as did Dorcas, back in that other Lydia's time.

The little cottage sorely needed a woman's touch. There were three babies—one, three, and five years of age—who were terribly neglected. When she went in, the poor mother, bedfast, wept tears of gratitude at her kind offer.

"You'll stay—until—until——" she faltered, tears bathing her thin face.

"Yes, dear, I will," promised Lydia, and she began what seemed to be an almost hopeless task of straightening up the snarls in the distressed household. Lydia learned another way of selling the fabric of kings—of kind words that are verily written in the Lord God's book of remembrance. She scrubbed till her soft, pretty hands looked as if they were parboiled. She kept the ironing board up constantly the first week, till she got the precious babies as clean as babies ought always to be. She prepared plain, nourishing foods, well cooked and delicately seasoned, for the wistful little mother. And at night, when the sick woman was wakeful and the pain was great, Lydia crept out of bed and rubbed the tortured arms and legs till the sufferer fell asleep. She had her pay a hundredfold in gratitude from the sad, patient husband, from the adorable clamoring babies, and from the sweet benediction of the Father above.

The night the little mother died Lydia promised her she would stay on until satisfactory arrangements could be made. With a sigh of relief and gratitude the little woman turned over and quietly went to sleep.

Lydia stayed about three weeks, caring for the babies and the home; then an auntie came—fat, loving, and comforting—to rear her brother's little children.

That week Lydia received her "call." It was to be with a hall effort in Baltimore. Later in the next summer she assisted the same evangelists in a tent effort.

It was all wonderful for the girl, and people loved her. It seemed that she walked right into people's hearts and stayed there.

One day near the middle of August, the heat was nearly

unbearable. The attendance at the meetings had fallen off somewhat, as whole families, seeking relief from the intense heat, had gone to the seashore. The sky looked a little odd in the afternoon, and it was getting black around the horizon. Great thunderheads seemed to hang suspended in the breathless air. People looked hopefully at the sky and predicted a break in the heat wave.

"Looks as if a big rain is coming!"

"Yes, and here's hoping this heat will let up!"

The storm broke right after dinner. Evangelist Walker, after looking at the clouds about noon, came into the living tent and said to his tent master:

"There's wind in those clouds. Soon as you get through eating, let's go tighten up the tent as fast as we can. If we don't it might blow away."

Then he told his wife and Lydia to come in and gather up the hymnbooks and put them under a big tarpaulin behind the piano so they would not get wet. Lydia was arranging the last of the books when the storm hit.

It was a near tornado. The air was full of debris—flying branches, boards, shingles, and papers. The tumult of the storm was fearful. With an angry roar it seized upon the big tent, wrenched it from its mooring stakes, and threw it to the ground, a snarl of ropes, poles, and canvas. Everyone escaped but Lydia. The storm was over in a few minutes, and a great group of men, kindly disposed, came down to help to right the tent. With a score or more to aid, it was not long till the poles were upright and the canvas was again creeping up the poles. A dozen men were tying ropes, pounding in stakes, and straightening chairs.

"Why, yer pianer's knocked over," shouted one of the men, who had been righting the chairs. Just then Mrs.

Walker rushed into the tent, her face as white as marble.

"John!" she screamed breathlessly, "where's Lydia?"

All the men looked at one another for an instant. Then the eyes of every one of them were drawn toward the piano lying on its back by the side of the platform.

"Oh, my!" breathed one of the men. "She's under that pianer!"

Lydia suffered no ill effects from her harrowing experience, much to the amazement of everyone. She passed out hymnbooks that very night and went right on with her Bible readings the next day. The whole town buzzed with the miracle of it. The tent was full that night, and Lydia could feel the wondering eyes of scores of people on her. Again she thought of Paul, contemporary with that other Lydia, who had said:

"In journeyings often, in perils of waters, in perils of robbers, in perils by mine own countrymen, in perils by the heathen, in perils in the city, in perils in the wilderness, in perils in the sea, in perils among false brethren; in weariness and painfulness, in watchings often, in hunger and thirst, in fastings often, in cold and nakedness." It was a great comfort to the girl to know that there was truly a loving watchcare over her, preserving her for some purpose known to the Infinite One.

All through that summer she did her precious Bible work joyfully, as unto the Lord. And the close of the effort saw a rich reward for all the labors in souls won for the kingdom.

The next summer she went with a tent effort to a great Eastern city. There were really two preachers. One was a practiced and finished city evangelist, and the other was a boy just out of college—a dark, silent young fellow, intelligent and earnest. Lydia noted that he was richly talented in music and in speaking, and folks everywhere predicted a brilliant future for him. He led the singing, took care of the tent, and preached one sermon a week. The evangelist was a big jovial fellow, and he took to teasing Lydia about his assistant. Then they would all laugh at her when the warm apricot color would tint her cheeks and ears.

"Ha!" he would laugh, "If only John Drummond could see you now, he'd feast his eyes more than he has been of late, which is aplenty!"

Then Lydia took to avoiding the young man, simply because she was teased so much. Anyway, she had such an embarrassing habit of blushing every time he looked her way.

Though she did not know it then, John was thinking a few thoughts himself. He couldn't help admiring the way her fair hair curled away from her forehead or the way her hands looked when she played the piano. But what he admired most about the girl was her deep spirituality. Her religion was a living, breathing, vital thing with her. Perhaps that was why she had such wonderful success with her Bible readings. She believed it, and believed it so earnestly that belief seemed to form an aura about her. It was infectious. People caught that belief in spite of themselves and laid hold on the blessed plow of God—not to lay it down until the kingdom will be ushered in.

Evangelist Bateman and his wife had rented a furnished apartment fairly near the tent, and John Drummond lived and batched in a small tent beside the big one. There was a dairy lunch nearby, where he got one meal a day.

Lydia had considerable difficulty finding a suitable

place for herself. She thought at first that she would get a room at the YWCA, but it was so far from the tent that transportation was a real problem. The Batemans let her sleep on their davenport till she could find the room she wanted. Either the price asked was too high for her slender purse or the place was so untidy that she felt that three of her five senses would be constantly violated were she to take the place.

One night, after a particularly exhausting day of giving Bible readings and answering advertisements for rooms, Lydia was pleasantly surprised when a woman stopped her at the back of the tent at the close of meeting. She had noticed the woman before. She was a pleasant-appearing woman, her hair and clothing neat. But there was a look, an indefinable something about her eyes and mouth, that Lydia did not like.

"Were you looking for a room, Miss Moore?"

"Why, yes—er, do you, that is, have you—I mean, do you know of a room near here?"

The woman smiled a little at Lydia, then replied, "I am a widow, Miss Moore. My name is Hardy—Amelia Hardy. I have a great big house a block down the street, and there is no one but me in all that house. Now, I have a big front room you can just as well stay in during your effort—no reason why you can't."

"Oh, but maybe I can't afford it, Mrs. Hardy! How much are you asking for your room? It would be so near and handy, but it seems as if I just can't afford a room to fit my pocketbook!"

"Afford, fiddlesticks!" laughed the woman.

"Why, I'm not going to charge you anything for my room! Dear, dear! Precious little missionary work I get done anyway, seems as if I'm so busy. Now there, dear. It'll be worth a whole lot to me to have you around. I get most awfully lonesome sometimes."

"Oh, but I couldn't possibly take it without paying you something. That wouldn't be right, you see. I'd have to pay any other place."

"Yes, but I'm not running a boardinghouse, Miss Moore. And I definitely do not need the money. My husband left me very comfortably fixed when he died, and I shall be glad to have you come. Here, my dear, is my card. You can have your things brought down tomorrow. Your room will be ready for you."

Then flashing Lydia a quick smile, the woman went away, leaving the girl with that vague feeling of dread and fear. She stood there for a moment pondering this. There was apparently no reason for this silly fear. Then she became aware that John Drummond was standing beside her. All the other people were gone. Even the evangelist and his wife had left to take an infirm old woman home. John had been fixing the tent for the night.

"What did that woman want of you?" he inquired, looking down into Lydia's fair young face.

"Why—why, she offered me a room at her house," she said, blushing to the very roots of her hair. "She said I could have it for nothing, and I could move in tomorrow."

John Drummond did not say anything for a moment. He looked off across the tent, his fine high forehead knit in puzzlement and worry.

"I can't explain it," he said at length, "but I somehow don't trust that woman. Something about her—I don't know just what—rings the warning bell in me. I wish you wouldn't go."

"I feel the same way, Mr. Drummond," said Lydia, "and even more so since you have told me your fears. I don't know why I feel so, myself. It's perfectly silly, and I suppose we'll both laugh at our foolish fears this time next week."

But John's face did not relax. "Just the same," he said, "I wish there was some way you could get out of going. I don't——"

"Listen!" whispered Lydia, her cheeks as red as roses. "There come the Batemans! I'll run and close the piano. If they see me talking to you they'll tease me to death!"

"I like to be teased about you, Lydia," answered John, boyishly, his brown eyes still on her. But Lydia fled up the aisle without answering, her heart thumping and her ears burning and a strange little happy flutter in her heart. "Was —was he only joking, or did he mean it?" she asked herself as she closed hymnbooks and shut down the lid of the old piano.

Then the Batemans came in, jolly and happy, and she went home. She told them of her offer, and even they were a little reluctant to let her go.

"Might as well stay here, Lydia," boomed Elder Bateman expansively. "Hate to see you go anyway. You're kind of a comfortable little person to have around. You keep us young."

But Lydia knew she was crowding them, and she laughed a little at their solicitations, even though a strange little fear kept tugging at her heart.

The next day John helped her move her things. The woman met them at the door and made every effort to have Lydia feel comfortable and at home.

The house was a great, heavy-browed brick affair with

a wide, old-fashioned veranda almost encircling it. There were wooden shutters at the windows, painted a dull moss green. Inside, the house was dark, even at midday. The rugs were dark and somber, the furniture was heavy and exuded a musty odor, almost "spooky," thought Lydia as she and John followed Mrs. Hardy up the wide mahogany steps. They were carpeted in dull green Brussels, and the upstairs hallway was the same.

Turning to the left, Mrs. Hardy advanced up the hall a few feet, then stopped, stooped over, and inspected a keyhole in the half light, unlocked the door, and swung it open. Lydia gasped in surprise. It seemed hardly possible that this lovely little gem of a room could possibly belong to this gloomy old house. It was as sunny as the rest of the house was gloomy. The furniture was bird's-eye maple, and the rug, lamp shades, draperies, and bedspread were old rose.

"This was my daughter's room," she said. "No one has slept here since she—passed on."

Again Lydia felt that sharp little fear. But this time it was tempered by pity.

"Oh!" she cried, "maybe I———"

"It's all right," the older woman said hoarsely. "You look like her. I'd like to have you occupy her room."

John carried her suitcases, and then went back after her brief case and hatbox while she straightened up her room and hung up her dresses.

John got back with her brief case and she finished putting things in the closet and in the dresser drawers. She had intended to take her meals at the little dairy lunch across the street, but the woman would have none of it.

"Just me in this big house, and you go out to eat!

Fiddlesticks! Why, Mary is always grumbling because I don't eat enough. She just revels in cooking for a crowd. You eat here, and welcome, my dear. Save your money for dresses and gloves and hats. You can afford to be a little vain. You're young only once!"

There was thick cream on her cereal in the morning, glasses of creamy milk, and eggs delicately cooked.

At night when she came home, tired from her day's work, her bed was always turned down and her night clothes were laid out. On her table always was a dish of fresh fruit—big peaches in blush-velvet dresses; grapes, frosty and filled with juice; and big oranges, fairly begging to be peeled and eaten in juicy sections. There was always a tray there, too, with a thin, delectable sandwich, a tiny dish of wafers, and a glass of fruit drink. It seemed that Mrs. Hardy was leaving no stone unturned to keep Lydia comfortable. But the girl could not get rid of that odd little fear.

One night when Lydia came home she chanced to notice some literature lying on the hall table. Idly curious, she picked it up and leafed it through. Then that warning bell rang again in her heart. Why—why, this was spiritualist literature! The girl stepped back and stooped over to look at the titles of some of the books in the bookcase. Spiritualist, spiritualist—every one of them.

Lydia felt her flesh fairly creep. Evangelist Bateman had only that night preached a fiery and powerful sermon against that modern form of devil worship. He had thundered against it. She had noted, too, that Mrs. Hardy had left while they were singing the closing hymn. She had not even waited for the benediction. Strange, she had never done that before.

Then, nervous as a cat, Lydia made her way up the gloomy stairs to her room. Her fears were real now, not simply imaginary. Every shadow seemed to be a living thing ready to jump out and pounce on her. Her fright was partially dissipated at the sight of her snowy bed, inviting and cool, and the tempting little tray on her table. Then Mrs. Hardy came in and visited awhile, cordial and pleasant, but Lydia could plainly see that she was terribly disturbed, even agitated. It was with a conscious effort that she carried on their little chatty conversation. Then she went to her room, and Lydia heard the key grate in the lock of her door. It had an eerie sound.

When Lydia went to bed that night she prayed a little longer and read more in her Bible than usual. Even then, as she lay there rigid, with the lights turned out, it seemed that the darkness was closing in upon her. She remembered her fears—John's fears. Tomorrow she would move. She would find some excuse to get out of this house with its queer noises, its threatening shadows, and this strange woman. She'd——

But her tired nature asserted itself, and Lydia fell into a troubled, uneasy sleep. It seemed that she had slept only a few minutes when she awoke suddenly with the sense of a great weight on her chest. She reached up and tore at it in an agony of fear. She could not breathe.

And then, in her dire extremity, she cried out to God to help her, as might one who is dying. Instantly the weight lifted. Years afterward Lydia was to talk of that experience and even then to lower her voice to a hushed whisper.

"The enemy was determined to destroy me," she would say, "because I was a 'seller of purple.' But the God of Paul and that other Lydia built a hedge about me."

With trembling fingers Lydia lighted the lamp and spent the remainder of the night in prayer and Bible study. Her terrible fear left her at the sweet assurance of the constant companionship of Christ and His holy angels.

The next morning Mrs. Hardy came to Lydia's door before she went down to breakfast. Her eyes had that particularly odd look about them that had repelled Lydia at the first.

"Do you have asthma, Miss Moore?" she asked pleasantly. "I was awakened last night by your—your hard breathing, and I wondered."

Instantly it came over Lydia that the woman was probing—trying to find out something. Looking her squarely in the eye, the girl said soberly:

"Mrs. Hardy, whenever I am in trouble I call upon the Lord, and He always hears me and helps me."

Instantly a change came over the woman. It was almost as if a mask were torn from her face. Her countenance became horrible to see. She began to scream and jump as if she were possessed with a legion of devils.

"You're going to be a medium, you little fool," she hissed. "I'll have you yet. I'll show you. I'll show you. I talked with the spirits last night. They said you——"

"Stop!" cried Lydia in a clear high voice. "Stop! I tell you I'll never, never be a medium. I'd rather die than be in fellowship with the devil."

And then the woman seemed to be possessed with demoniacal rage. She threw herself onto the floor and writhed and screamed and screeched and yelled. The very air seemed to be moving with the spirit of wickedness. Lydia watched her, terrified and unmoving for some time. Then the doorbell pealed through the house. Lydia drew a sigh of relief. Never had anything sounded so good in her whole life. She ran past the hysterical woman, down the stairs, and threw open the door.

It was John, blessed John, his kind face sober, and his big brow knit with worry.

"I was worried about you, Lydia," he said. "I had a strange feeling that you were in trouble or danger or something. The Batemans laughed at me, but——"

Lydia's cup was running over. She burst into a torrent of weeping. John came in, puzzled and concerned, and took her trembling hands.

"Why, Lydia, is something the matter? What is it? Tell me, Lydia!"

"L-let's get away f-from this terrible place," she sobbed. "And th-then I'll tell you. Come up and get my suitcase. I'll have it packed in just a moment."

As they ascended the stairs they heard Mrs. Hardy go into her room and lock her door. In ten minutes they were out on the street.

"Lydia," said John, "I was terribly worried about you. I was sure you were in grave danger. I could hardly wait until a decent hour to come and see about you."

It came over the girl how utterly sweet it was to have someone concerned over her, to have someone care. And John was so big and tall and handsome. She liked the way that big heavy wing of black hair smoothed back from his forehead, and she liked his kind eyes.

Then, while they were walking back to the tent, she told him of her harrowing experience. He whistled, and they looked back at the house in the distance.

"A spiritualist medium!" he muttered. "Well, you surely had reason to be afraid."

At the end of the beautiful summer they saw many of the people for whom they had labored baptized in a placid lake nearby. Then Lydia went home to Philadelphia for the first time in nearly three years. She wondered a little as to what her reception would be, for her mother had not seemed to waver a bit in her decision. But mother love is strong and does not die easily. When Lydia came into the bakery, her mother was arranging some fresh bread on the shelves. When she turned around, Lydia looked at her.

Sarah Moore gave a low cry and fairly flew around the counter to her child.

"O Lydia, my sweet, my precious!" she wept. The two of them clung together, laughing, crying, and kissing each other.

"Kathleen! Chester!" Mrs. Moore cried out at length, "come see who's here!"

Lydia got a chance that night to talk a little with her mother about religion. But her mother anticipated her.

"I've been kinda readin' the Scripture, Lydia, and I don't know but what you're right. Why, I was mad as a hornet, Lydia, and wanted to set you and Granny right, but I guess I——"

"You got set right yourself, didn't you?" and Lydia laughed softly.

"Yes, and I'm takin' studies from the Martins you used to know. I'm goin' to close my bakery on Saturdays and open it Sundays."

Then Lydia told her mother of John.

"And, Mother, he has had a call to evangelistic work in the South. He wants me to go with him. I came home to visit awhile before I go. He is coming next week. I want you to meet him. He's wonderful!"

"Lydia," said her mother with sudden inspiration, "why don't you go up to Granny's to get married? I'll go with you. She sets such store by you. I never saw the like. It'll tickle her to pieces. We'll go downtown tomorrow and get your outfit. I'll call in Miss Higgins to sew. You shall have as pretty a wedding gown as any in town."

To please Mother and Granny, she had a white satin wedding dress.

John came the day they were to start north. Lydia was proud to introduce him to her folks. He was so tall, so gracious, and so dignified, yet he was jolly and friendly, and they loved him immediately.

Mother left a cousin in charge of the store, and they all took the train north. The Martins were coming the next day.

The wedding was sweet and beautiful. Granny decked the whole parlor of her homely little house with great fluffy chrysanthemums that she had grown in her own garden. The old woman had a certain amount of stiff artistry about her that made the old-fashioned room strangely beautiful. She even insisted on playing a quaint old-fashioned wedding march on the tall, ornate reed organ for them to come in by. Her stiff, twisted old fingers achieved the musical gymnastics admirably, and she looked so pleased when Lydia peeped over the banisters at her that Lydia felt the tears sting her eyelids.

Then almost before she knew it she found herself at John's side, facing the minister. John took her arm and looked down at her. "You little darling!" he whispered, as the chords of the wedding march faded away.

"Dearly beloved, we are gathered together——" "Oh! He is marrying us," thought Lydia, her vagrant thoughts running ahead of the beautiful text of the ceremony. Then one glance at the tall figure beside her, and she brought her thoughts back forcibly to the issue at hand. The minister was asking her a question.

"Do you take this man to be your lawfully wedded husband, and wilt——" Well, it didn't matter what he asked her to promise as far as dear John was concerned. She would go with him to the ends of the earth in this wonderful work of winning souls.

It seemed only a moment before the ceremony was over, and they were surrounded by a happy, laughing group. But little, vital Granny fairly dominated the scene. She kissed her new grandson and Lydia tenderly.

"I know that thee will be happy," she stated proudly. "For thee has the most beautiful work in all the world. But don't thee forget," and she shook a rheumatic old finger at John playfully, "that thee is not the only preacher. Lydia beat thee to the trade by three long years."

We invite you to view the complete
selection of titles we publish at:

www.TEACHServices.com

scan with your mobile
device to go directly
to our website

Please write or email us your praises, reactions, or
thoughts about this or any other book we publish at:

P.O. Box 954
Ringgold, GA 30736

Info@TEACHServices.com

TEACH Services, Inc., titles may be purchased in bulk for
educational, business, fund-raising, or sales promotional use.
For information, please e-mail:

BulkSales@TEACHServices.com

Finally if you are interested in seeing
your own book in print, please contact us at

publishing@TEACHServices.com

We would be happy to review your manuscript for free.

www.ingramcontent.com/pod-product-compliance
Lightning Source LLC
Chambersburg PA
CBHW021026090426
42738CB00007B/922